Travel Etiquettes for the Sacred Journey of Ḥajj

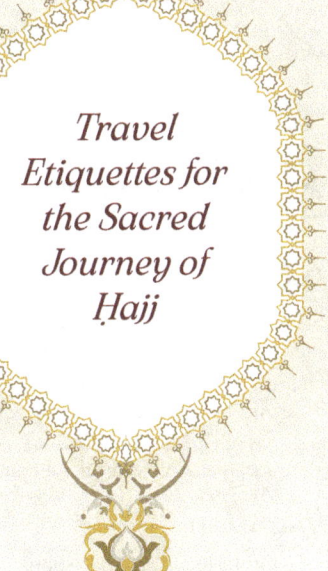

Ḥajj is a fundamental pillar of 'Islām that carries immense reward and countless blessings. To attain these rewards and blessings, it is necessary to fulfill this obligation properly, in accordance with the sharī` ah–especially since, for many, it is a once-in-a-lifetime opportunity.

The following checklist is designed to help you attain as many blessings as possible from this sacred journey, 'in shā' Allāh.

Settle Debts and Trusts

Settle all debts and return any entrusted items to their rightful owners.

Make Up All Obligations

Fulfill all missed prayers, zakāh, and fasts. Repent sincerely for past shortcomings. Make a firm intention to avoid missing any future obligations and to refrain from committing sins.

Seek Permission

- Seek permission from those whose consent is required to travel, such as parents or a husband.
- If you are in debt and currently unable to repay your creditors, their consent should also be obtained.
- If permission is not granted, one should still try their utmost to gain their forgiveness. However, ḥajj remains permissible.

Pure Intention

The intention for the journey of ḥajj should be solely to please Allāh Ta` ālā and the beloved Messenger of Allāh, may Allāh send blessings and salutations upon him.

Maḥram for Women

A woman is required to travel with a maḥram if she intends to travel more than 57.2 miles from her home. If she performs ḥajj without one, her ḥajj is valid, but she will be sinful for violating this condition.

Ḥalāl Earnings

Ensure that you are fulfilling the obligation of ḥajj through ḥalāl earnings, as ḥajj may not be accepted otherwise.

Means to the Knowledge and Rulings of Ḥajj

Carry a basic fiqh manual, or travel in the company of a reputable ` ālim (scholar). At the very least, keep a reliable guidebook on hand. A recommended option is The Ḥajj Guide by Mufti Sayyid 'Asad al-Qādirī and Mufti Salmān al-Nūrī.

When Departing

- Request du` ās from your loved ones– you will attain blessings through them.
- Seek forgiveness from your family and friends.
- Leave your family under the divine protection of Allāh and entrust Him with their safety, well-being, and wealth.
- Recite durūd sharīf in abundance–not only upon departure, but throughout the sacred journey. It comes in a ḥadīth: "Whoever forgets to send blessings upon me has erred in the path to Jannah."

During the Journey

- Avoid wasting time. Stay focused and avoid unnecessary sightseeing or distractions.
- Return with gifts or tabarrukāt from the Ḥaramayn.
- Most importantly, offer the gift of du` ās to all your loved ones.

Ḥajj Supplications

When Departing

Recite the prescribed du`ā for the safety of your family and belongings:

اللَّهُمَّ إِنَّا نَعُوذُ بِكَ مِنْ وَعْثَاءِ السَّفَرِ وَكَآبَةِ الْمُنْقَلَبِ وَسُوْءِ الْمَنْظَرِ فِي الْمَالِ وَالْأَهْلِ وَالْوَلَدِ

'al-lā-hum-ma 'in-nā na` ū-dhu bi-ka min wa` -Thā-'is-sa-fa-ri wa ka-'Ā-ba-til mun-qa-la-bi wa sū-'il man-ẓa-ri fil-mā-li wal-ah-li wal-wa-la-di

"O Allāh, we seek refuge in You from the difficulty of travel, the burden of return, and the evil eye within the wealth, family, and offspring."

When Traveling

Recite the prescribed du`ā for the safety of your family and belongings:

سُبْحَانَ الَّذِيْ سَخَّرَ لَنَا هَذَا وَمَا كُنَّا لَهُ مُقْرِنِيْنَ وَإِنَّآ إِلَى رَبِّنَا لَمُنْقَلِبُوْنَ

sub-ḥā-nal-la-dhī sakh-kha-ra la-nā hā-dhā wa mā kun-nā la-hū muq-ri-nīn wa 'in-nā 'ilā rab-bi-nā la-mun-qa-li-būn

"Exalted is He who put this [vehicle] under our control while we were incapable, and indeed we all will surely return to our Lord."

When Ascending Any Height

اللّٰهُ أَكْبَرُ

'al-lā-hu 'ak-bar

"Allāh is the greatest."

When Descending Any Height

سُبْحَانَ الله

sub-ḥā-nal-lāh

"Glory be to Allāh."

When Disembarking the Airport

أَعُوذُ بِكَلِمَاتِ ٱللّٰهِ ٱلتَّامَّاتِ كُلِّهَا مِنْ شَرِّ مَا خَلَقَ

'a`ū-dhu bi-ka-li-mā-ti-l-lā-hit-tām-māti kul-li-hā min shar-ri mā kha-laq

"I seek refuge in all the complete words of Allāh from all the evil amongst His creation."

At the Mīqāt

After praying two units (rak`ah), recite the appropriate intention (nīyah) based on the type of ḥajj you are performing:

1 - For Mufrid (Only Ḥajj)

اللّٰهُمَّ إِنِّي أُرِيْدُ الْحَجَّ فَيَسِّرْهُ لِي وَتَقَبَّلْهُ مِنِّيْ
نَوَيْتُ الْحَجَّ وَأَحْرَمْتُ بِهِ مُخْلِصًا لِلّٰهِ تَعَالٰى

'al-lā-hum-ma 'in-nī 'u-rī-dul-ḥaj-ja fa-yas-sir-hu lī wa ta-qab-bal-hu min-nī na-way-tul-ḥaj-ja wa 'aḥ-ram-tu bi-hī mukh-li-ṣan lil-lā-hi ta` ā-lā

"O Allāh, indeed I am intending ḥajj. So, make it easy for me and accept it from me. I intended ḥajj and I entered the state of 'iḥrām for it, sincerely for Allāh, the Exalted."

2 - For Mutamatti` (`Umrah first, then Ḥajj)

اللّٰهُمَّ أُرِيْدُ الْعُمْرَةَ فَيَسِّرْهَا لِيْ وَتَقَبَّلْهَا مِنِّيْ
نَوَيْتُ الْعُمْرَةَ وَأَحْرَمْتُ بِهَا مُخْلِصًا لِلّٰهِ تَعَالٰى

'al-lā-hum-ma 'u-rī-dul-`um-ra-ta fa-yas-sir-hā lī wa ta-qab-bal-hā min-nī na-way-tul-`um-ra-ta wa 'aḥ-ram-tu bi-hā mukh-li-ṣan lil-lā-hi ta` ā-lā

"O Allāh, I am intending `umrah. So, make it easy for me and accept it from me. I intended `umrah and I entered the state of 'iḥrām for it, sincerely for Allāh, the Exalted."

3 - For Qārin (`Umrah and Ḥajj together)

اللَّهُمَّ إِنِّي أُرِيدُ الْعُمْرَةَ وَالْحَجَّ فَيَسِّرْهُمَا لِي وَتَقَبَّلْهُمَا مِنِّيْ
نَوَيْتُ الْعُمْرَةَ وَالْحَجَّ وَأَحْرَمْتُ بِهِمَا مُخْلِصًا لِلَّهِ تَعَالَىٰ

'al-lā-hum-ma 'in-nī 'u-rī-dal-`um-ra-ta wal-ḥaj-ja fa-yas-sir-hu-mā lī wa ta-qab-bal-hu-mā min-nī na-way-tul-`um-ra-ta wal-ḥaj-ja wa 'aḥ-ram-tu bi-hi-mā mukh-li-ṣan lil-lā-hi ta`ā-lā

"O Allāh, indeed I am intending `umrah and ḥajj. So, make them easy for me and accept them from me. I intended `umrah and ḥajj and I entered the state of 'iḥrām for them, sincerely for Allāh, the Exalted."

Talbiyah

لَبَّيْكَ اللَّهُمَّ لَبَّيْكَ لَبَّيْكَ لَا شَرِيكَ لَكَ لَبَّيْكَ إِنَّ
الْحَمْدَ وَالنِّعْمَةَ لَكَ وَالْمُلْكَ لَا شَرِيكَ لَكَ

lab-bay-ka al-lā-hum-ma lab-bayk, lab-bay-ka lā sha-rī-ka la-ka lab-bayk, 'in-nal-ḥam-da wa nni`-ma-ta la-ka wal-mulk, lā sha-rī-ka lak

"Here I am, O Allāh, here I am. You have no partner, here I am. Indeed, all praise, blessings, and sovereignty belong to You—You have no partner."

- *From the time you wear your 'iḥrām until the ramī of Jamrah, recite talbiyah abundantly.*
- *Men should recite the talbiyah loudly—but not so loud that it distracts others.*
- *It is not permissible for women to raise their voices in talbiyah such that it is heard by non-maḥrams. However, they should recite it in a tone audible to themselves.*

At Mad` ā

This area is known to be the place where the Holy Ka`bah was visible when there were no buildings blocking it.

Make du`ā and seek forgiveness for all your relatives and loved ones.

Recite durūd sharīf in abundance and this prescribed du`ā:

اَللّٰهُمَّ هٰذَا بَيْتُكَ وَأَنَا عَبْدُكَ أَسْأَلُكَ الْعَفْوَ وَالْعَافِيَةَ فِي الدِّيْنِ وَالدُّنْيَا وَالآخِرَةِ لِيْ وَلِوَالِدَيَّ وَلِلْمُؤْمِنِيْنَ وَالْمُؤْمِنَاتِ وَلِسَيِّدِنَا الْكَرِيْمِ صَدْرِ الشَّرِيْعَةِ أَمْجَدْ عَلِيْ، اَللّٰهُمَّ انْصُرْهُ نَصْرًا عَزِيْزًا، آمِيْنَ.

'al-lā-hum-ma hā-dhā bay-tu-ka wa 'a-nā
`ab-du-ka 'as-'a-lu-kal-`af-wa wal-`ā-fi-ya-ta
fid-dīn wad-dun-yā wal-'ā-khi-ra-ti lī wa
li-wā-li-day-ya wa lil-mu'-mi-nī-na
wal-mu'-mi-nā-ti wa li-say-yi-di-nal-ka-rīm
ṣad-rish-sha-rī-`a-ti 'am-jad `a-lī
'al-lā-hum-man-ṣur-hu naṣ-ran `a-zī-zan, 'Ā-mīn

"O Allāh, this is Your House and I am Your slave. I ask You for forgiveness and well-being in religion, in this world, and in the hereafter—for me, my parents, the believing men, the believing women, and for our noble master Ṣadr al-Sharī`ah 'Amjad `Alī. O Allāh, grant him a mighty victory. 'Āmīn."

When Entering Bāb al-Salām

أَعُوذُ بِاللهِ الْعَظِيمِ وَبِوَجْهِهِ الْكَرِيمِ وَسُلْطَانِهِ
الْقَدِيمِ مِنَ الشَّيْطَانِ الرَّجِيمِ بِسْمِ اللهِ الْحَمْدُ لِلَّهِ
وَالسَّلَامُ عَلَى رَسُولِ اللَّهِ اللَّهُمَّ صَلِّ عَلَى سَيِّدِنَا
مُحَمَّدٍ وَعَلَى آلِ سَيِّدِنَا مُحَمَّدٍ وَأَزْوَاجِ سَيِّدِنَا مُحَمَّدٍ
اللَّهُمَّ اغْفِرْلِي ذُنُوبِي وَافْتَحْ لِي أَبْوَابَ رَحْمَتِكَ

*'a`ū-dhu bil-lā-hil-`a-ẓī-mi wa
bi-waj-hi-hil-ka-rīm wa sul-ṭā-ni-hil-qa-dīm
mi-nash-shay-ṭā-nir-ra-jīm bis-mil-lāh al-ḥam-du
lil-lāh was-sa-lā-mu `alā ra-sū-lil-lāh
'al-lā-hum-ma ṣal-li `alā say-yi-di-nā
mu-ḥam-mad wa `alā 'ā-li say-yi-di-nā
mu-ḥam-mad wa 'az-wā-ji say-yi-di-nā
mu-ḥam-mad 'al-lā-hum-magh-fir lī dhu-nū-bī
waf-taḥ lī ab-wā-ba raḥ-ma-tik*

"I seek refuge in Allāh, the Almighty, His divine presence, and His eternal kingdom from the accursed Shayṭān. Allāh's name to begin with — all praise is due to Allāh — and salutations be upon the Messenger of Allāh. O Allāh, send blessings upon our master Muḥammad, upon the family of our master Muḥammad, and the wives of our master Muḥammad. O Allāh, forgive my sins and open for me the doors of Your mercy."

When Exiting the Masjid

أَعُوذُ بِاللَّهِ الْعَظِيمِ وَبِوَجْهِهِ الْكَرِيمِ وَسُلْطَانِهِ الْقَدِيمِ
مِنَ الشَّيْطَانِ الرَّجِيمِ بِسْمِ اللَّهِ الْحَمْدُ لِلَّهِ وَالسَّلَامُ
عَلَى رَسُولِ اللَّهِ اللَّهُمَّ صَلِّ عَلَى سَيِّدِنَا مُحَمَّدٍ وَعَلَى آلِ
سَيِّدِنَا مُحَمَّدٍ وَأَزْوَاجِ سَيِّدِنَا مُحَمَّدٍ اللَّهُمَّ اغْفِرْلِي
ذُنُوبِي وَافْتَحْ لِي أَبْوَابَ فَضْلِكَ وَسَهِّلْ لِي أَبْوَابَ رِزْقِكَ

'a`ū-dhu bil-lā-hil-`a-ẓīm wa bi-waj-hi-hil-ka-rīm wa sul-ṭā-ni-hil-qa-dīm mi-nash-shay-ṭā-nir-ra-jīm bis-mil-lāh al-ḥam-du lil-lāh was-sa-lā-mu `alā ra-sū-lil-lāh 'al-lā-hum-ma ṣal-li `alā say-yi-di-nā mu-ḥam-mad wa `alā 'ā-li say-yi-di-nā mu-ḥam-mad wa 'az-wā-ji say-yi-di-nā mu-ḥam-mad 'al-lā-hum-magh-fir lī dhu-nū-bī waf-taḥ lī ab-wā-ba fa-ḍlik wa sah-hil lī ab-wā-ba riz-qik

"I seek refuge in Allāh, the Almighty, His divine presence, and His eternal kingdom from the accursed Shayṭān. Allāh's name to begin with — all praise is due to Allāh — and salutations be upon the Messenger of Allāh. O Allāh, send blessings upon our master Muḥammad, upon the family of our master Muḥammad, and the wives of our master Muḥammad. O Allāh, forgive my sins, open for me the doors of Your grace, and ease for me the doors of Your sustenance."

Intention of Ṭawāf

اللّٰهُمَّ إِنِّيْ أُرِيْدُ طَوَافَ بَيْتِكَ الْمُحَرَّمِ
فَيَسِّرْهُ لِيْ وَتَقَبَّلْهُ مِنِّيْ

'al-lā-hum-ma 'in-nī 'u-rī-du ṭa-wā-fa bay-ti-kal-mu-ḥar-ram fa-yas-sir-hu lī wa ta-qab-bal-hu min-nī

"O Allāh, indeed I intend the ṭawāf of Your Sacred House. So make it easy for me and accept it from me."

When Doing 'Istilām of the Black Stone (Ḥajar 'Aswad)

Raise your hands up to your ears, palms facing the Black Stone, and recite:

بِسْمِ اللّٰهِ وَالْحَمْدُ لِلّٰهِ وَاللّٰهُ أَكْبَرُ
وَالصَّلَاةُ وَالسَّلَامُ عَلَى رَسُوْلِ اللّٰهِ

bis-mil-lāh wal-ḥam-du lil-lāh wal-lā-hu 'ak-bar waṣ-ṣa-lā-tu was-sa-lā-mu `a-lā ra-sū-lil-lāh

"Allāh's name to begin with. Praise belongs to Allāh. Allāh is the greatest. Blessings and salutations be upon the Messenger of Allāh."

When Proceeding to Walk for Ṭawāf

اللّٰهُمَّ إِيمَانًا بِكَ وَاتِّبَاعًا لِسُنَّةِ نَبِيِّكَ
مُحَمَّدٍ صَلَّى اللّٰهُ تَعَالَى عَلَيْهِ وَسَلَّمَ

'al-lā-hum-ma 'ī-mā-nan bi-ka wat-ti-bā-`an li-sun-na-ti na-biy-yi-ka mu-ḥam-mad ṣal-lal-lā-hu ta-`ā-lā `a-lay-hi wa sal-lam

"O Allāh, [I begin Ṭawāf] with faith in You and following the sunnah of Your Prophet Muḥammad (may Allāh's blessings and salutations be upon him)."

Du`ā at Every Point Around the Ka`bah

Du`ās for every point reached during ṭawāf of the Ka`bah have been recorded by earlier scholars. However, due to the large crowds nowadays, they are often difficult to recite in full. Therefore, it is best to recite durūd at every point, as the acceptance of du`ā is guaranteed through it.

Sayyidī 'A`lā Ḥaḍrat states:
"One should make du`ā when passing in front of the Multazam, Rukn `Irāqī, Mīzāb al-Raḥmah, and Rukn Shāmī. There are special du`ās prescribed for each of these points, which have been quoted in Jawāhir al-Bayān Sharīf. However, as these du`ās may be difficult to read, one should instead recite that which the Messenger of Allāh, may Allāh send blessings and salutations upon him, has promised acceptance and greatness for, and that is sending durūd and salām upon the Beloved Prophet, may Allāh send blessings and salutations upon him."

('Anwār al-Basharah)

When Approaching the Mustajāb

This area lies between the Rukn Yamānī and Rukn 'Aswad. Seventy thousand angels are appointed here to say 'Āmīn to every du`ā made.

Make du`ā for yourself and your loved ones here. Even reciting durūd sharīf is sufficient.

You may also recite the following du`ā:

اللّٰهُمَّ هٰذَا بَيْتُكَ وَأَنَا عَبْدُكَ أَسْأَلُكَ الْعَفْوَ وَالْعَافِيَةَ فِي الدِّيْنِ وَالدُّنْيَا وَالآخِرَةِ لِيْ وَلِوَالِدَيَّ وَلِلْمُؤْمِنِيْنَ وَالْمُؤْمِنَاتِ وَلِسَيِّدِنَا الْكَرِيْمِ صَدْرِ الشَّرِيْعَةِ أَمْجَدْ عَلِيْ، اللّٰهُمَّ انْصُرْهُ نَصْرًا عَزِيْزًا، آمِيْن.

'al-lā-hum-ma hā-dhā bay-tu-ka wa 'a-nā `ab-du-ka 'as-'a-lu-kal-`af-wa wal-`ā-fi-ya-ta fid-dīn wad-dun-yā wal-'ā-khi-ra-ti lī wa li-wā-li-day-ya wa lil-mu'-mi-nī-na wal-mu'-mi-nā-ti wa li-say-yi-di-nal-ka-rīm ṣad-rish-sha-rī-`a-ti 'am-jad `a-lī 'al-lā-hum-man-ṣur-hu naṣ-ran `a-zī-zan, 'Ā-mīn

"O Allāh, this is Your house and I am Your slave. I ask You for forgiveness and well-being in religion, this worldly life, and the hereafter—for me, my parents, the believing men, the believing women, and for our noble master Ṣadr al-Sharī`ah 'Amjad `Alī. O Allāh, grant him a mighty victory. 'Āmīn."

At Maqām Ibrāhīm

وَاتَّخِذُوا مِنْ مَّقَامِ إِبْرَاهِيمَ مُصَلًّى

wat-ta-khi-dhū mim-ma-qā-mi 'ib-rā-hī-ma mu-ṣal-lā

"And make the standing place of 'Ibrāhīm a place of prayer."

After Praying Two Rak` ahs of Ṭawāf

اللّٰهُمَّ إِنَّكَ تَعْلَمُ سِرِّي وَعَلَانِيَتِي فَاقْبَلْ مَعْذِرَتِي وَتَعْلَمُ حَاجَتِي فَأَعْطِنِي سُؤْلِي وَتَعْلَمُ مَا فِي نَفْسِي فَاغْفِرْ لِي ذُنُوبِي، اللّٰهُمَّ إِنِّي أَسْأَلُكَ إِيمَانًا يُبَاشِرُ قَلْبِي، وَيَقِينًا صَادِقًا حَتَّى أَعْلَمَ أَنَّهُ لَا يُصِيبُنِي إِلَّا مَا كَتَبْتَهُ لِي، وَرِضًى مِنَ الْمَعِيشَةِ بِمَا قَسَمْتَهُ لِي، يَا أَرْحَمَ الرَّاحِمِينَ

'al-lā-hum-ma 'in-na-ka ta`-la-mu sir-rī wa `a-lā-ni-ya-tī faq-bal ma`-dhi-ra-tī wa ta`-la-mu ḥā-ja-tī fa-'a`-ṭi-nī su'-lī wa ta`-la-mu mā fī naf-sī fagh-fir lī dhu-nū-bī 'al-lā-hum-ma 'in-nī 'as-'a-lu-ka 'ī-mā-nan yu-bā-shi-ru qal-bī wa ya-qī-nan ṣā-di-qan ḥat-tā 'a`-la-ma 'an-na-hū lā yu-ṣī-bu-nī il-lā mā ka-tab-ta-hū lī wa ri-ḍan mi-nal-ma-`ī-sha-ti bi-mā qa-sam-ta-hū lī yā 'ar-ḥam-ar-rā-ḥi-mīn

"O Allāh, indeed You know my confidential and public matters, so accept my excuse. And You know my needs, so grant me what I ask. And You know whatever is in my heart, so forgive my sins. O Allāh, I ask You for such faith that my heart rejoices and wholeheartedly accepts, until I know with certainty that nothing will afflict me except what You have written for me, and that I am content with the provision You have decreed for me. O the Most Merciful of those who show mercy."

After Drinking Zamzam

يَا وَاجِدُ يَا مَاجِدُ لَا تُزِلْ عَنِّيْ نِعْمَةً أَنْعَمْتَهَا عَلَيَّ

yā wā-ji-du yā mā-ji-du lā tu-zil `an-nī ni`-ma-tan 'an-`am-ta-hā `a-lay-ya

"O the Finder, O the Glorifier, do not remove the blessing You have bestowed upon me."

While Ascending the Stairs of Ṣafā

Engross yourself in dhikr and durūd sharīf.

Intention of Sa`ī

اللّٰهُمَّ إِنِّي أُرِيدُ السَّعْيَ بَيْنَ الصَّفَا وَالْمَرْوَةِ فَيَسِّرْهُ لِي وَتَقَبَّلْهُ مِنِّي

'al-lā-hum-ma 'in-nī 'u-rī-dus-sa`-ya bay-naṣ-ṣa-fā wal-mar-wa fa-yas-sir-hu lī wa ta-qab-bal-hu min-nī

"O Allāh, indeed I am intending sa`ī between Ṣafā and Marwah, so make it easy for me and accept it from me."

During Sa`ī

Stay engaged in tasbīḥ, takbīr, ḥamd, thanā', and durūd throughout the sa`ī.

When Approaching the Green Lights (Mīlayn al-'Akhḍarayn)

Recite the following:

رَبِّ اغْفِرْ لِيْ وَارْحَمْنِي وَأَنْتَ الْأَعَزُّ الْأَكْرَمُ

rab-bigh-fir lī war-ḥam-nī wa 'an-tal-'a-` az-zul-'ak-ram

"My Lord, forgive me and have mercy on me. You are the Most Mighty, the Most Noble."

Whenever Your Sight Falls Upon the Ka` bah

Recite the following three times:

لَا إِلٰهَ إِلَّا اللّٰهُ وَاللّٰهُ أَكْبَرُ

lā 'i-lā-ha 'il-lal-lā-hu wal-lā-hu 'ak-bar

"There is no deity except Allāh, and Allāh is the greatest."

While Traveling to Minā

Recite the talbiyah, durūd sharīf, and thanā' in abundance.

When Minā Becomes Visible

اَللّٰهُمَّ هٰذِهِ مِنٰى، فَامْنُنْ عَلَيَّ بِمَا مَنَنْتَ بِهِ عَلٰى أَوْلِيَائِكَ

'al-lā-hum-ma hā-dhi-hi mi-nā fam-nun `a-lay-ya bi-mā ma-nan-ta bi-hi `alā 'aw-li-yĀ-'i-ka

"O Allāh, this is Minā, so bestow upon me whatever You have bestowed upon Your chosen servants."

The Day of ʿArafah

After Fajr, remain engaged in talbiyah, dhikr, and durūd sharīf.

While Proceeding to ʿArafah

Clear your heart and mind of distractions, as this is the day your ḥajj may be accepted or rejected. Avoid unnecessary conversation.

Engage abundantly in:

Durūd Sharīf *Dhikr* *Talbiyah*

Upon Seeing Jabal al-Raḥmah

Increase your dhikr, durūd sharīf, and talbiyah, as this is a moment of great hope — as it is, 'in shā' Allāh, a time of acceptance.

Wuqūf al-`Arafah

Spend as much time as possible making du`ā and avoid wasting time. This is a moment designated by Allāh Ta`ālā for du`ā — do not squander it on worldly distractions. Remain engrossed in du`ā, dhikr, durūd, and reciting the Qur'ān until sunset. Try to shed tears, as it is a sign of acceptance. If that is not possible, keep a sorrowful expression.

Recite this prescribed du`ā in `Arafah:

اللّٰهُمَّ هَذَا بَيْتُكَ وَأَنَا عَبْدُكَ أَسْأَلُكَ الْعَفْوَ وَالْعَافِيَةَ فِي الدِّيْنِ وَالدُّنْيَا وَالآخِرَةِ لِيْ وَلِوَالِدَيَّ وَلِلْمُؤْمِنِيْنَ وَالْمُؤْمِنَاتِ وَلِسَيِّدِنَا الْكَرِيْمِ صَدْرِ الشَّرِيْعَةِ أَمْجَدَ عَلِيٍّ، اللّٰهُمَّ انْصُرْهُ نَصْرًا عَزِيْزًا، آمِيْنَ.

'al-lā-hum-ma hā-dhā bay-tu-ka wa 'a-nā
`ab-du-ka 'as-'a-lu-kal-`af-wa wal-`ā-fi-ya-ta
fid-dīn wad-dun-yā wal-'ā-khi-ra-ti lī wa
li-wā-li-day-ya wa lil-mu'-mi-nī-na
wal-mu'-mi-nā-ti wa li-say-yi-di-nal-ka-rīm
ṣad-rish-sha-rī-`a-ti 'am-jad `a-lī
'al-lā-hum-man-ṣur-hu naṣ-ran `a-zī-zan, 'Ā-mīn

"O Allāh, this is Your house and I am Your slave. I ask You for forgiveness and well-being in religion, this worldly life, and the hereafter—for me, my parents, the believing men, the believing women, and for our noble master Ṣadr al-Sharī`ah 'Amjad `Alī. O Allāh, grant him a mighty victory. 'Āmīn."

While Departing to Muzdalifah

Engross yourself in dhikr, durūd sharīf, talbiyah, and weeping throughout the journey.

In Muzdalifah

Spend the entire night in dhikr, durūd sharīf, talbiyah, and weeping.

While Departing to Minā

Remain engaged in dhikr, durūd sharīf, and talbiyah.

When Arriving at Wādī al-Muḥaṣṣar

اللّٰهُمَّ لَا تَقْتُلْنَا بِغَضَبِكَ وَلَا تُهْلِكْنَا
بِعَذَابِكَ وَاعْفُ عَنَّا قَبْلَ ذٰلِكَ

'al-lā-hum-ma lā taq-tul-nā bi-gha-ḍa-bi-ka wa lā tuh-lik-nā bi-`a-dhā-bi-ka wa`-fu `an-nā qab-la dhā-lik

"O Allāh, do not execute us by Your wrath, and do not destroy us with Your punishment, and pardon us before that."

When Minā Becomes Visible

اَللّٰهُمَّ هٰذِهِ مِنٰى، فَامْنُنْ عَلَيَّ بِمَا مَنَنْتَ بِهِ عَلٰى أَوْلِيَائِكَ

'al-lā-hum-ma hā-dhi-hi mi-nā fa-mnun `a-lay-ya bi-mā ma-nan-ta bi-hi `alā 'aw-li-yĀ-'i-ka

"O Allāh, this is Minā, so bestow upon me whatever You have bestowed upon Your chosen servants."

At the Jamrah

بِسْمِ اللهِ اللهُ أَكْبَرُ

bis-mil-lā-hi al-lā-hu 'ak-bar

"In the name of Allāh — Allāh is the greatest."

After Performing Qurbānī

Make du`ā for the acceptance of your own ḥajj and the ḥajj of all Muslims.

Removing or Trimming the Hair

Start from the right side and recite:

اللهُ أَكْبَرُ اللهُ أَكْبَرُ لَا إِلٰهَ إِلَّا اللهُ
وَاللهُ أَكْبَرُ اللهُ أَكْبَرُ وَلِلّٰهِ الْحَمْدُ

'al-lā-hu 'ak-bar 'al-lā-hu 'ak-bar lā 'i-lā-ha 'il-lal-lā-hu wal-lā-hu 'ak-bar 'al-lā-hu 'ak-bar wa li-l-lā-hil-ḥamd

"Allāh is the greatest, Allāh is the greatest. There is no deity except Allāh, and Allāh is the greatest, Allāh is the greatest, and for Allāh is all praise."

Additional Supplications

When Losing Something

يَا جَامِعَ النَّاسِ لِيَوْمٍ لَا رَيْبَ فِيهِ، إِنَّ اللهَ لَا يُخْلِفُ الْمِيعَادَ، اجْمَعْ بَيْنِي وَبَيْنَ ضَالَّتِي

yā jā-mi-`an-nā-si li-yaw-min lā ray-ba
fī-hi 'in-nal-lā-ha lā yukh-li-ful-mī-`ād
'ij-ma` bay-nī wa bay-na ḍāl-la-tī

"O the Gatherer of mankind for the day in which there is no doubt — indeed Allāh does not break His promise. Unite me and my lost possession."

When Drinking Zamzam

اللَّهُمَّ إِنِّي أَسْأَلُكَ عِلْمًا نَافِعًا وَرِزْقًا وَاسِعًا وَعَمَلًا مُتَقَبَّلًا وَشِفَاءً مِنْ كُلِّ دَاءٍ

'al-lā-hum-ma 'in-nī 'as-'a-lu-ka `il-man nā-fi-`an
wa riz-qan wā-si-`an wa `a-ma-lan
mu-ta-qab-ba-lan wa shi-fā-an min kul-li dā-in

"O Allāh, indeed I ask You for beneficial knowledge, abundant sustenance, accepted deeds, and a cure from every illness."

www.ingramcontent.com/pod-product-compliance
Lightning Source LLC
Chambersburg PA
CBHW061723120626
46550CB00003B/1342
* 9 7 8 1 9 5 7 7 7 3 1 4 8 *